MY LIFE

ISN'T

FLOWERS

A JOURNEY
THROUGH
POETRY
AND
PICTURES

Poetry, art work, and photography by

Sasha Wolfe

Sasha Wolfe
152 Pleasant View Road
Bradford, NH

sashawo@tds.net
www.sashawolfe.net

Copyright 2008 by Sasha Wolfe

All rights reserved. No part of this book may be reproduced in any form or by electronic or mechanical means including information storage and retrieval systems without permission from the author, except by a reviewer, who may quote brief passages in a review.

All photographs and other artwork are by Sasha Wolfe except for the two of the author.

Book information:

Wolfe, Sasha
    My Life Isn't Flowers: a journey through poetry and pictures / Sasha Wolfe
    ISBN: 978-0-578-00164-7
    1. Poetry. 2. Writing. 3. Photography. 4. Art. 5. Self-realization.

ACKNOWLEDGEMENTS

Where do I start? I am thankful for so much, to so many.

My mother, Marge, is the critic and keeps me humble. She provides the nest, yet forces me to fly.
Without her, I don't know where I'd be.

Old Friends:
To Anne, my poetry reading partner and second mother; we have shared laughter, life stories, Tai Chi, and quite a few tears. She encourages me to do this. I owe her much.

To Gail, sister I never had and childhood mentor, who returned after many years and pushes me to succeed. She continues to support and advise me and she's always there when I need her.

To Lou, who loved and supported me when I needed it most.

To Paulette, my Ladies of Leisure partner, who walked many a lonely shore with me and introduced me to Goose Rocks Beach in Kennebunkport.

New Friends:
Everyone I have met since moving to Bradford has been welcoming, but there are a few who hold special places in my heart.

To Betty, who from the start, was here for Ma and I. She convinced me to get back into healing, introduced me to the artisans' fairs, and she and Nelson have been indispensable.

To Valerie, another sister of my soul and fellow adventurer; I thank her for the wonderful conversations. She is an inspiration in positive thinking.

To Holly, an inspiration, for sure; unwilling to give in to age, in her eighties, she's still on the go.

To Deborah, who led me to the writing group. We have many great discussions.

To Joan, Gayle, Lynne, and Perley--- more writing supporters. Their different styles make the group pleasant and interesting and that allows each of us to explore where the writing takes us.

To Kate D, who supports my groups at the Community Center. We have wonderful conversations.

To Kate J, who joyfully passes out my business cards and sends me clients.

To John, Clara, and Mike who have graciously allowed me to photograph their barns

Training-teachers:
Every interaction is an opportunity to learn and some lessons have been easy while others have been quite difficult. When it comes to "professional" training, four names come to the fore:

To Dennis (Jampal), who put me in front of the class and the huge mirrors, taught me centering, grounding, and Tai Chi while using me as his assistant/demonstrator. For one petrified of being in front of a group, this taught me self-confidence and allowed me to realize that one such as I could have grace and beauty.

To Master Mantak Chia who gave me the Healing Tao Instructor's certificate through which other doors opened.

To Claire, who taught a unique and powerful form of leadership. The few years I spent affiliated with the Women's Center brought me to a new level of self awareness.

To Spotted Wolf, who is taking me into a new realm and through whom came my spirit name.

There have been many others who have played an important role in my healing. Writers who have led the way: David Whyte's poetry and audios opened the door for me to discover the joys of digging in my well, Julia Cameron who gave me permission to be an artist, and Natalie Goldberg who instructs everyone to "keep the pen moving." For years I listened to the words of Marion Woodman, Clarissa Pinkola Estes, Robert Bly, and Angeles Arrien--- and there have been and will be many more…

TABLE OF CONTENTS

Acknowledgements	7
Pictures	11
Introduction	13
My Life Isn't Flowers (poem)	

Chapter 1: Life Along the Ocean — 16

Aftermath	17
Another Rescue	18
Apathy	19
Dawn's Early Light	20
Downward Spiral	21
Dreaming the Sea	22
Escape to the Sea	23
Fog Bank	24
How Can I Not Love the Sea?	25
How Do You Draw the Sea	26
Humility's Lesson	27
Inner Morsels	28
Remnants of Summer	29
Sand Dollars Price	30
Soul Death	31
Starfish Treasure	32
Storm Wake	33
Stretching Time	34
Summer Day	35
Turn of the Tide	36

Chapter 2: Finding Joy — 37

Full Blinding Brilliance	38
I Want to Live	39
Loved by the Earth	40
Magic and Light	41
Of Golden Fields	42
Pause	43
Reflections on Watermelon	44
The Moment of Possibility	45

Chapter 3: Explorations in Creativity — 46

Cooking Lessons	47
Creative Desire	48
Creative Pool	49
Creative Urges	50
Creativity Pours	51
Different Desires	52
Dreaming the Peach	53
Hunger	54
Whoops!	56

Chapter 4: Relationships--- Self, Other, and Spirit   57
    "I Think Therefore…"   58
    Accusations   59
    Burn   60
    Clinging to Memory   61
    Craving Validations   62
    Ode to My Friends   63
    Echo of Days Gone By   64
    Floyd's Wrath   65
    Future's Past   66
    I Give With Joy   67
    No Excuse   68
    Open Heart Surgery   69
    Pieces of You   70
    Remembered Sounds   71
    Response   72
    Savored Words   73
    See No Evil   74
    Tell Me   75
    The Gathering   76
    "…Therefore I Am"   77

Chapter 5: In Meditation   78
    Beyond Silence   79
    Embrace   80
    Exploring Emptiness   81
    Insomnia   82
    Lightning Strike   83
    Pre-Dawn Tai Chi   84
    Shopping   85
    Stand In Silence   86
    Telling   87
    I.   88
    II.   89
    VI.   90
    VII.   91
    VIII.   92
    IX.   93
    X.   94
    XI.   95
    XII.   96
    XIII. Purpose and Intent   97
    XIV.   98
    XV. The Waiting   99
    XVI. Letting Go Identity   100
    XVII. Walking Meditation   101
    XIX. Calling Windhorse   102

Chapter 6: 103
    #1 104
    2 105
    3,4 106
    5 107
    6,7 108
    8 109
    9 110
    10 111

In Closing: 112
    Purpose 113
    They Will Never Write Songs About Me 116

About the Author 117

PICTURES

    Bunch o' Daisies   15

Chapter 1: Life Along the Ocean
    Glistening Sands in the Pre-dawn   16
    Aftermath   17
    Ocean's Sculpture   18
    Dawn Glistening Sands   20
    Foggy Shoreline   21
    Goose Rocks Dune   22
    Sunrise Greeting   23
    Melted Horizon   24
    Arrangement by Waves   25
    Constant Movement   26
    Mesmerized   27
    Bow Tie   28
    Seaweed Littered Shore   29
    Fluffy White Centers   30
    Windswept Fences   31
    Dawning Brilliance   35
    Remnants   36

Chapter 2: Finding Joy
    Boardwalk O'er the Dunes   37
    Colors of Dawn   38
    Sedona   39
    Closer to Yellow   41
    Fuzzy Soft Grasses   42
    Awaiting the Glory   43
    The Moment of Possibility   45

Chapter 3: Explorations in Creativity
    Midnight Dreaming, oil on canvas, combo, 1999   46
    Moon Setting Over Meadow, charcoal landscape, 2008   47
    Sitting With Dragonflies, acrylic on slate, 1997   48
    Waters Edge, oil on canvas combo, 2001   49
    Todd Reflections, charcoal landscape, 2008   50
    Hawk Landing on Branch, photo 2008   51
    Freyja, photo 2008   52
    Lily Deep, photo 2007   53
    Poetry Reading Aboard Ship   56

Chapter 4: Relationships--- Self, Other, and Spirit
    Priceless Expressions   57
    Full Moon Reflected on the Bellamy   58
    Raging Storm Clouds   59
    Fiery Reflections in the Pre-Dawn   60
    Alone on the Boardwalk   61
    Winter's Silence   62
    In a Field of Black-eyed Susans   63
    Daisies and…   64

Transformation of Lilies	69
Walking the Water's Edge	70
Crashing Wave	71
Connection	73
Out to Pasture	74
Grand Canyon North Rim	75
Heaven's Dancing	76
Snow on the Mountain	77

Chapter 5: In Meditation

Barred Contemplation	78
Stairway to Emptiness	79
Sedona Colors	80
With Head Bowed	81
On the Darkened Pond	82
Hayloft	83
Drawn Into Orange	84
Almost Forgotten	85
Lines and Angles	87
Watchful	88
Solitary Contemplation	89
Forgotten Wheels	90
Playa del Carmen Sunrise	91
Adoration	92
Twisted Cat	93
Heavenly Still	94
Caught in the Bath	95
Lily-of-the-Valley	96
Butterfly Dance on Purple Asters	97
Beyond Repair	98
Power lines at Dawn	99
Budding Details	101
Greetings	102

Chapter 6: Letting the Words Flow

Following	103
For Ever Greens	104
Abandoned	105
Reflections In And Out	106
Close Up	107
Into the Fog	108
Layers of Sunflower	109
Wooden Peg	110

In Closing

One Last Look	112
Autumn Colors	115
Earrings & Things	115

About the Author

Sasha at the easel	116

INTRODUCTION

Friends have been pushing me to do another book for ten years and I've finally taken the time. But how does one choose from a decade worth of poems? What do I want to tell? These are my babies, cries from deep within my soul that I've allowed to come to the light, and shouts of joy. Do I dare share them and let them be criticized? Will you understand?

Writing has been my salvation, my therapy, and the expression of my deepest emotions. Through poetry, I have been able to let go of much grief and I've discovered wonder and awe in the flow of unedited words. There's something about letting creativity pour forth without judgment that allows healing and joy, and once the words are on the page, I then allow time for adjustments.

Poetry comes out of fragmented thoughts. Sometimes the words are triggered by an event or something said, but other times, the words just stream into my consciousness and I have to write them down. Great peace is found in the release as if I am cleaning heart, mind and soul. The words looking back from the page allow me to see where I've been and help me understand who I am. What is most amazing is that, when I allow the words to flow, I never know where the poem will end up. I'm often very surprised. It's like finding buried treasure.

The trick, however, is in taking the time to pick up the pen. If I don't do so immediately, the words slip away and are forever lost as that initial feeling fades. The muse is impatient; if I don't pay attention when she comes, she disappears, and that precious moment cannot be called back.

I have a deep connection to the earth and hours are spent walking solitary trails and shorelines with camera, pens and notebook at the ready. Many poems have come during these walks. It's as if the earth and sky are giving something back to me as I am pouring my heart out into the fresh air.

As with poetry, I have been taking pictures for many years learning as I go. I never arrange settings but will take the photograph as the scene appears. There is much beauty around us and I want to share the joy, the awe, and the peace of such moments. I often crop my pictures to get close to the subject or to enhance the scene. My wish is to share the beauty of life whether it's an intricate flower or a dilapidated barn.

The goal of this book is to share the sorrows and joys of life, and although many of the poems seem sad, (after all, they did come out of grief,) the writing of them brought me such joy. By sharing my pain, I have allowed light to reach the darkest parts of my soul. By sharing my words, I hope to reach you so that you are not so alone in your times of darkness. I cannot tell you how freeing it has been to write these poems! I want this book to be more than just a poetry read. I want my words to touch you, to inspire you to pick up the pen and let your own words flow. Who cares if it's drivel! The act of writing will open your awareness and teach you more about life than you can imagine.

Life is not only about hard times. Joy abounds also and the natural beauty around us is so inspiring! There's the self discovery found in meditation and other healing arts. We need to feed the creative fires within to heal and be free, and we need to channel those flames onto page, canvas or whatever medium our creative desires call forth or we will burn up inside and become numb.

So grab your picks and shovels, gather your brooms and handi-wipes, and go into your inner wells and start cleaning. Get out some tools or find your brushes and pens and let your creativity bubble forth.

CLEANING DAY IN THE WELL

On the inside of my soul lies a darkened place
and stuck in an unused corner like burnt cheese
is….something… possibly sinister…
I cannot tell for sure

It's been covered over so many times
that I have forgotten much of what I've buried
and I don't know what has oozed
into the hidden recesses of my being
to rot and grow hard

But I have this handy dandy scraper now
a plastic little thing that will not scar the sides
(came with a George Foreman grill
that my ex gave me many years ago
and I no longer use)

So down there I go
with my handy dandy scraper and cleaning rags
I pick and scrub with care
wipe away the grime and the dust and the char
to reveal… a mirror

With gentle strokes I wipe the surface clean
then, with a silent bang, light reflects in the shine
and I am no longer in the dark
I am bathed in glorious sunlight
and all is revealed

Yea yah.

David Whyte, my favorite poet, talks about going into the well to work on healing. Through the years, I have been able to feel this well inside me and it has been very interesting to, once in awhile, go in there and stir the gunk around.

This poem that I wrote started as a picture in my mind of a little me climbing down the ladder with that plastic scraper. I put the pen to the page and the poem practically wrote itself. I didn't know where it would go and what a surprise to uncover that mirror!

    I chose, for the title of this book, the poem, "My Life Isn't Flowers," from the need to explain some of my poems. My very good friend, Anne, has written many wonderful poems about flowers and the beauty of nature, but for me, life goes much deeper. My mother claims that many of my poems are too sad, but for me, being able to put feelings into words brings such joy; it's a release of the darkness that has been harbored in my soul. Once those emotions are released, I am able to bring more light into my being and peace to my heart.
    Please, enjoy the poems and the pictures.

MY LIFE ISN'T FLOWERS

My life isn't flowers
but that's okay
my words seldom
speak of sweet bouquets

Instead I feel
my way along
with words that sing
emotional songs

Life is lived
with ups and downs
I call it, I see it
the wheel goes 'round

Healing is found
in the truth of words
speak to me
you'll always be heard

Because that's what we do
when words we share
we help one another
we show that we care

My life isn't flowers
but that's okay
I take what I'm given
and then give it away.

I have been given a new name, a spirit name
and was told to add the name
to this book.

It is with great joy that I announce
that my spirit name is

CRYING HEART

because my heart cries
for the beauty of this earth
and I want all people
to experience
the beauty and joy
as I see it

CHAPTER 1: LIFE ALONG THE OCEAN

I shall always love the ocean
the majestic healing powers
of a long, lonely shoreline
and the sound of the crashing waves

Many hours
days upon days
I wandered in solitude
cried a thousand tears
died a hundred deaths

Through the beauty
and the wonder
I survived

For some, the poems in this first chapter may seem sad. This was a point in my life where I was very unhappy in my job. I was training in the healing arts and my new beliefs were at war with the corporate atmosphere of the work place. Though much relief was found in taking long walks, it came to pass that the decent salary, six weeks vacation, and good benefits could not outweigh the daily misery on the job. After 27 ½ years, I was able to quit that job and the ensuing year was spent in healing.

My intent is not to make you feel sad or think that I am miserable. There were times, but the joy in the beauty of nature cannot be denied and at the end of my sabbatical, I was able to find a job where I had a boss who taught me how to laugh again. I count my blessings every day for these opportunities.

AFTERMATH

The ocean's
Ominous churning up
Of seaweed and sand
High tide
Waters today
Too inhospitable
To touch
Only to be watched
From a distance

Wave upon
Continuous wave
Crashing roar
Deafening rumble
Small seagulls
Feast amongst
Dying seaweed
One eye kept
On the surge

Sands once
Walked upon
Have been
Carried away
In last night's
Wind and surf
Leaving
Cliffs and pits
Along a beach
Once flat

I alone
Chance this day
And forage
With the gulls
For interesting
tidbits

ANOTHER RESCUE

I wandered
from the water's edge
lost my soul
to the dying and dead

In sunlight shadow
I crept and shivered
from factory glare
I simmered and quivered

Back to the sea
to find relief
walking the shore
cast off my grief

Moonlight rising
I release my pride
tears flow freely
death passes by

Another day rescued
by the sand and the sea
I shall always give honor
to Her gloriously

APATHY

Empty wrappings
styrofoam cups
litter the ground
among cigarette butts

Napkins blow
across unmowed grass
catch in dandelions
clover and sassafras

Beside the pond
trash forms a ring
where butterflies hover
and grasshoppers sing

I sit at a table
stained with burns
write this ditty
while my stomach churns

And at my feet
to the debris and the butts
I think I'll add
by throwing up.

I have an issue with litter. I just don't understand how people can trash a place of beauty; how anyone can be so thoughtless. We all see it, though. It's a part of this society. So sad.

I spent a lot of time trying to come up with a poem and though I don't write many rhyming poems, this somehow seemed appropriate.

DAWN'S EARLY LIGHT

The sea paints
A beautiful picture
On wet sand canvas
Splashed
With the color
Of dawning skies

I am caught
Between time
And the shoreline
Awaiting the moment
Of pure brilliance
That will release
My wintering soul
Into the cosmos
Of possibility

Blinded,
My eyes drop

Before me
The glistening
Orange, pink, gold sands
Awaken a desire
To rush off
And create
A perfect day.

DOWNWARD SPIRAL

Too wrapped
In present crisis
To enjoy the morn
I am closed
To the pounding
Surf

Her crashing waves
Cannot break
These locks
Nor seagull cry
Wake me from
This apathy

Yet the call
Still answered
I trudge
These lonely
Shores
Stiff and achy
Body as immovable
As the spiraling
Descent
Of my mind.

DREAMING THE SEA

I think I shall always
love the sea
Once
after the moonlight
faded
I chased shadows
across the sands
til the receding tide
caught my attention

I walked with the gulls
in the crisp breaking waters
til the sand dollar
called my name

I could not tell
if I was dreaming
or if everyday
was the true illusion

I felt alive!
I was aware of everything
til the tiny grains of sand
in my shoes
reminded me
of a small, lonely girl

I longed to run
barefoot
in the surf.

ESCAPE TO THE SEA

I long for the solitude
Of a long, lonely beach
Where there is
Nothing or no one
Coming at me
But the sun, the sand
And the sea

Where the only sound
Is the roar of the surf
And cry of seagulls
Fighting over
Bits of crab

Where the smaller terns
Run down the shoreline
Ahead of me
In a synchronized group
Forming a wave
Of their own

I want to lie
On the beach
Let the sands
Wrap me
In their earthly blanket
While the sun
Fills me
With healing warmth

I want to,
For a few brief moments,
Forget I live
Anywhere else.

FOG BANK

This is how I like it
when the gray
of the sky
meets the gray
of the horizon
and the sun
is a veil
shaped behind
the rolling cloud

You cannot tell
where the sea ends
or the heavens begin

You cannot tell
if the illusion is reality
or if walking out
into the waters
will accomplish anything

With days like these
solitude Is everything
and the always active mind
continues its search
for peace

With days like these
solitude Is everything
and the always active mind
continues its search
for peace.

HOW CAN I NOT LOVE THE SEA?

How can I not
love the sea
when She paints
such beautiful pictures

I can not leave
a beach such as this

Wave after wave
whooshing down
on one another
hiss across the sand
the roar drowning out
every other sound
even the mindless chatter
in my head

I search the shoreline
for trinkets, photograph
shells and seaweed
arranged as only the waves
can leave them

I catch the flight
of the seagulls
in the camera lens
and follow along
in the wake of terns

How can I
not love the sea
when She lays
such breathtaking
pictures before me?

HOW DO YOU DRAW THE SEA

How do you draw the sea
the rippled waves
the crashing foam
sun-wet rocks

Surely those who come
are hypnotized
by Her resounding
rhythm

Surely those who come
are mesmerized
by Her illusive
dreaming

How do you draw the sea
when your own
inner oceans
are drowning
in a pool of inactivity
and you do not know
which way to turn
or who to count on

Surely those who come
are stymied
by your empty
pages

Surely those who come
are confused
by your blocked
creativity

How do you draw the sea
when you cannot
match your waves
to Hers?

HUMILITY'S LESSON

What lesson, this humility
To contain intoxicated emotions
In a washed up seashell
Feelings screaming for justice
Heart crying for peace
Mind stilling the tongue

What price, this humility
To bear daily frustrations
With weary smile, gentle movement
 Coming and going in silent acceptance
While waves crash thunderous
Disapproval at my apathy

How wears this humility
When I have forgotten how to forgive
Compassion being the unreachable light
At the end of the tunnel
And I am left dripping at the water's edge
As the receding wave carries away my soul

How speaks this humility
When I only have myself to feed
From bits and pieces left behind
By hungering seagulls
And the ever changing tide returns
Again and again to fill my empty womb

INNER MORSELS

Being this close
To the waters
The lawn is
Covered by
Broken shells
Dropped by
Seagulls
Attempting
To get at
The soft inner
Morsels.

In practice,
I, too
Drop from
Above

The awareness
To break through
My hardened
Cold heart
To set free
The love and
Compassion
Buried within

My heart
As empty
As those
Left over shells
Fills with
Possibility
And light

I offer
The pieces,
My own soft
Inner morsels
To the wind

REMNANTS OF SUMMER

Outgoing tide
Leaves behind
Seaweed covered beach
Smell of dying
Assails the senses
As I trudge
In the footsteps
Of yesterdays'
Thousands

Remnants
Of a passing summer
Lay claim
On tomorrow
Seen today
In debris
Washed up
From a society
Wasting away
On greed,
Unconsciousness,
And ego

Part of me dies, too
And pieces
Of my heart
Are left amongst
Seaweed wrapped litter.

SAND DOLLAR'S PRICE

I may never
know why
the price
for my words
is one solitary
sand dollar

My tongue
laps the shoreline
for every
morsel

The pickings
are plentiful
for others
but the round
starred discs
do not come
to me
until
I've poured
from my heart
a thousand
useless
words

SOUL DEATH

In pre dawn light
Seagulls circle
Over a field
Black against gray
Like vultures
Eyeing the dying

I look for
A carcass
But see only
My own
Lying in sodden grasses
Empty of eyes
That no longer see

My soul has died
Turned in on itself
And I climb steps
To a workplace
That has picked
The bones clean
And has sucked
Life from the marrow

I would
Change all this
If I had any strength left
But the truth
Has been silenced
From my parched lips

STARFISH TREASURE

Holding the tiny body
in my open palm
trying to stop him
from curling
occasionally straightening
each arm
turning him
to lie flat

I wondered
if death for us
is as similar
lying in hospital bed
while others
turn us
position us
deny us
watch us
die

My mind
fell in the chasm
between right and wrong
I held a life
in my hand
I watched the tiny legs
wave against
the light of dawn
made excuses
that didn't quite justify
taking a life

But still, I
brought him home
made a strange place
for him to die
among other treasures
I have collected

Just like a doctor
just like a man

I went through a lot of emotions in the writing of this poem. I hated taking a life; hated myself for continuing to do that and yet, mesmerized by what was going on within me--- just because I wanted a starfish. Still, I made a choice I was not totally happy with. It was almost as if I was compelled to go through this experience.

I am hesitant to include the poem in this collection, as I do feel ashamed, but I have decided that perhaps this needs to be said, perhaps we need to be made aware of the choices we make and the consequences.

STORM WAKE

Drawn to the sea
As if a magic cord
Was tied to my waist
As if all the sea
Had to do
Was give a tug
And I'd come

Mesmerized
As wave after
Relentless wave
Pounds the shore
As if the waters
Themselves
Were trying to eat
Away the sands
To get to me

But the murky waters
Hold no magic today
I have no desire
To dive into
That angry sea

But I hear Her plight
As she coughs up
Beer bottles, coke cans
And fishing line
Onto a shore
Already littered
With dying seaweed
And half eaten fish

I can do nothing
But lay my heart
Alongside Hers
And weep.

STRETCHING TIME

Summer dreams
the windswept surf
onto the rocky shore
where solitary footprints
carve momentary fragments
into timeless eternity

The next wave
erases the passing
but the haunting cry
of a hungry gull
echoes across the sand
recalling yesteryears'
tormented memories

Searching for a new reality
I try to follow the footprints
before they wash away
on the incoming tide
The waves chant
their soothing melody

Breathe deep
breathe soft
whispers the sea
over and over

Breathe deep
breathe soft
til the sound
reverberates through
my mind, body and soul
and there is nothing left
but the crash of wave
cry of gull
and an endless
stretch of sand

Breathe deep
breathe soft

breathe deep
breathe soft

breathe deep
breathe soft

SUMMER DAY

Sun's warmth
brightness
after days of rain

Early morning wind
refreshing
creates a perfect day

Crashing waves
relentless
perform a comfort song

Lovers stroll
enjoying
the quiet of the morn

Writers write
poetic
of days like these

Til beachgoers
swarm like
an angry hive of bees

Peaceful morning
broken
time to move along

Back to wherever
we came from
back to where we belong

TURN OF THE TIDE

Somehow
I am
The empty beach
My mind
The thousands
Of footsteps
Across the sands
My body
The littered
Shoreline
Of forgotten
Memories

Yesterday's dreams
Washed up
Lie dying
In the sun
As the sea
Endlessly
Erodes the soul
And then
Rebuilds it
Again and again
In the subsequent
Turn of the tides.

CHAPTER 2:   FINDING JOY

I turn to nature to heal and
as the beauty of nature seeps into my awareness,
I become peace.

FULL BLINDING BRILLIANCE

Sun crested horizon
Brilliant, deep orange
Mesmerized
I stand naked
Before the window
My soul
Ripped open
To the splendor

Tantalizing colors
Expand my mind
And at the moment
Of complete fullness
The cloak
of dawning drops
Revealing full blinding
Brilliance

In heightened
Anticipation
I await the embrace
Of pure golden
Essence.

I WANT TO LIVE

I refuse to give this
Just to the morning
Though I love mornings
I want to carry
This freshness, this aliveness
To the end of the day

I want to lie down
With inspiration
As my bed mate,
I want to dream of tomorrows
Perched on a mountaintop
And have the morning sacredness
Merge with the late afternoon sun

I want to breathe in
Cool mountain air,
Lap crystal clear streams,
Run naked through green fields
Still wet with dew
And fill my soul with aromas
Of nature at Her best

I want to roll on a sandy beach
Right up to the surf's edge
While waves crash down around me,
Sit in a wooded glade
Basking in a spot of sun
Or lie on a freshly mowed lawn
Watching puffy white clouds
Against bright blue skies
While birds sing their lullabies

I want to hear, see, taste, smell, touch
I want to LIVE!

LOVED BY THE EARTH

I dream
Of beautiful green fields
Fresh in a spring-day sun
A tantalizing roll
Under soft breezes
Ripples across the sea
Wave after wave

Silken, sweet essence
Invades my senses
My entire being filled
With the splendor
Laid out before me
As the Great Mother
Seduces my womanhood
I feel I am
About to explode

I want to
Run, jump
Shout with joy
Skinny dip in this sea
Of undulating ecstasy

I want to lie down
Let hundreds of thin fingers
Caress my naked body
Massage my weary bones
Soothe my tired soul

I dream
Of sweet reeds
Tickling my aching flesh
Cupping my full, round breasts
Sweeping across my fat belly
To stroke the inside of my thighs

Breathless I lie
On the warm ground
Lips moist from Her kisses
Basking in golden sunlight
While waves of golden grasses
Sing me lullabies.

MAGIC AND LIGHT

I want to be Magic and Light
feel the energies ripple
across my skin to yours

I want to give what I cannot hold
and wave flowers across
my mother's breasts

I want to rise above what I am
climb mountains of stone
swim with dolphins

I want to forget pain and prejudice
wave my arms, kiss the boo-boos
make everything all right

I want this energy I feel so strong
to reach you in the dark
calm your fears

I want to know that you know
that it is all right and you
and I are of one breath

I want to be the magic and light
that I feel…

OF GOLDEN FIELDS

I used to love the fields
of late summer, early autumn.
Back then I would
haul off and wade
through grasses up to my thighs
never minding
that there might be ticks,
snakes or other creepy crawlees.

My mind would be open
and I'd investigate
every gully, every hill.
I would pick
Queen Anne's Lace, goldenrod
and brown eyed susans.
I'd run my hands
along the smooth bark of sumac
and touch the fuzzy red fruit clusters.

I'd lie among the grasses
pretending that those
who hunted me
would never see me.
Then I would roll onto my back
and let the clouds carry me away.

I remember the smells
of the grasses turned gold or purple topped,
the humming sounds of bees
and grasshoppers in flight
and the sun beating down
on my barely clad body.

That was my world, back then.
Now I look across lively meadows and wish…

PAUSE

Already pre-dawn skies
Are lighter
A precursor
To the coming
Of spring
And warmer weather

Bright silver sliver
Of a crescent
Hangs on the edge
Of the color change
As night
Gives way
To morning

I am caught
Somewhere between
The rising moon
And coming dawn
And who's to know
If I become lost
And never come back?

Who's to know
That I've given in
To the glory
Of the Universe
The smell of fresh air
And the brilliance
Of a sunrise?

Who's to know
That I've paused
In this morning's rush
Before the hurrying on
Into the metallic tasting
Man-made environment
Of the place I work?

REFLECTIONS ON WATERMELON

Summer swelter
My body drenched
I reach for the last slice

Bright and pink
My tongue probes the seeds
'Til they fall into my mouth

The boys see
Who can spit the farthest
But I am just a girl

Instead, after ridding my seeds
"Like a girl"
I once more let my tongue

Delve into the depths
Breaking off pieces
To dissolve in my mouth

Mmmm. sticky, sweet nectar
Dribbles down my chin
Onto my fingers

Succulent and wet
Oh, sooo cool in my mouth
Sooo refreshing

After the last swallow
I slowly run my tongue
Along the rind

Savoring any last juice
Then… one… by… one…
I suck…
my fingers…
dry

THE MOMENT OF POSSIBILITY

In this time, this moment
I ooze possibility
Oh, Spirit
Let me manifest these desires
Let my hands mold
the ideas like clay
Let form be created
as passion flows
like a roaring river.

In this time, this moment
I ooze possibility
Oh, Spirit
Let me fill to the brim
til the floodgates crash open
and words tumble
over each other
in their hurry
to get to the page
Let the ink in my pen
run as smooth as my thoughts.

In this time, this moment
I ooze possibility
Oh, Spirit
Let no excuse surface
to dam these gushing waters
Let my entire being
cascade with the joy
of creativity
Oh, Spirit
Let me remain open
til the last drop
is wrung
from my soul.

CHAPTER 3: EXPLORATIONS IN CREATIVITY

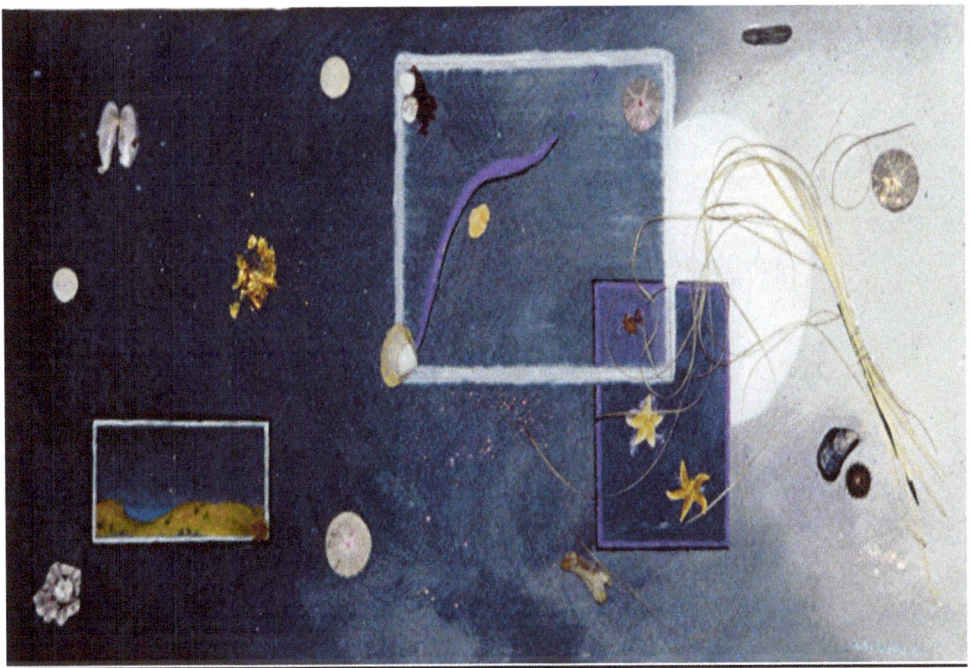

MIDNIGHT DREAMING

This was the first of my combo pieces.
Oil on canvas with additions.

    Of course I have to write about creativity. My life revolves around projects and ideas, poems and photography, drawing and painting. My motto is: "What is it and what can I make with it?"

    Creativity, though, often takes a back seat to other issues in life and when I cannot make the time to work on my art, frustration sets in and I become over emotional. That's when some of the poetry comes forth; a release of pent up emotions. At times it's been just enough to hang on…

    In this chapter, I've also included painting combos (multi-media), acrylic on slate, and charcoal landscape drawings.

COOKING LESSON

There is
Something
About solitude
That generates
Words

Something
About loneliness
That opens up
The well

From which
Flows
Uncooked parts
Of the self

The page
Becomes
The frying pan
And the words
Must be
Flipped
Ever so
Carefully
So they don't
Burn.

Charcoal drawing of the view from my back yard

CREATIVE DESIRE

Flooded
With creative
Desire
My bones
Awaken
Fingers stretch
For brush
For pen
Feet dance
To the rhythm
Of another
Dawn
And my mouth
Opens
To the songs
Of spring.

SITTING WITH DRAGONFLIES

Acrylic on slate. 1997

    The actual painting looks better than the photograph. My mother will tell you that I made one for all my friends, but never one for her.

CREATIVE POOL

For a person who writes
I believe everyone
should write

Why don't they see
the beauty in words?

Why can't they feel
the healing that comes
from allowing thoughts
into the Light?

Why don't they
understand
self awareness
can be revealed
on the written page?

Perhaps the potter
believes everyone
should love clay
Maybe the painter
wants everybody
to be in awe of color

I dunno.
I am easily
attracted to it all
and I dive in
joyful at getting
wet.

CREATIVE URGES

I am filled
The creative urges
Spiral through
My body
Flow through
My veins

My hands
Yearn to grasp
Pens and brushes
Allowing dreams
To manifest
On page or canvas

My hands
Pulse with
Pounding energy
To touch, to heal
To become One
With All that is
Sacred

So strong
This desire
My heart
Bleeds.

CREATIVITY POURS

Creativity
Doesn't stop
It pours
Through my veins
Like running water

Creating
Re-creating

Bubbling up
From my soul
Looking out
Through my eyes
Wars with my ego
To take over

Give me a chance
Take a few moments
It begs
And when I allow
I am
Fulfilled.

Hawk coming to land on a branch overhead. There were two flying about and I took numerous shots to get this one.

Notice the light coming through the tips and edges of the feathers.

DIFFERENT DESIRES

My creative desire
Alive in early morning
Is with pen and paper

Her desire
Is in the satisfaction
Of curiosity
And the excitement
Of bird watching

I try to sit
In silence
While the words
Pour forth

She crouches
By the window
Cackling at chickadees,
Tries to climb
The walls
And cries
At the unseen

My focus interrupted
By her restlessness
My attention
Given over
To her needs
I lay down
My pen
To play.

DREAMING THE PEACH

Finding words
To explain the emotions
The pen touches the page
while the mind wanders
the darkened valleys of my soul
searching for the key
that will unlock buried treasures

A picture forms
a peach
soft, ripe, fuzzy-skinned
one attached leaf
lapping at my quivering heart

Like that aged fruit
my body has turned to mush
but perhaps the flavor
will cause surprising words
to bubble up the throat
dance on my tongue and
between my teeth

Maybe my mind
will reach a straw
into the moist depths
and slowly sip its way
to dreaming

This was an exercise in choosing a subject, putting the pen to the page and writing. As usual, I had no idea where the writing would take me.

I don't have a picture of a peach, so decided to put in a photo of an orange lily.

The following poem came from my exploration with creative hunger and what happens if we don't allow ourselves freedom to create. It's important that we allow some kind of art into our lives. As we are created beings, we need to be creative in order to cope with daily stress.

HUNGER

I.

Hunger.
Ah, yes. Hunger.
The burning ignited within
that you try to quell
with food.

You eat and eat,
but the hunger
isn't satisfied.
You try to quiet it
with more food,
but still
it doesn't go away.

Sometimes
you think about it,
this hunger,
but what it says
scares you.
It reminds you
of dreams not fulfilled,
of projects not completed,
of ideas never brought to life.

A hunger
that at times
burns with such intensity
that it makes you cry,
makes you feel crazy
and you continue
to dampen the flame
with food
hoping you can sleep.

II.

Sometimes
The flame does diminish
(enough food
will weigh anything down)
and you wander days
like a zombie
hiding your feelings and desires
allowing the will of others
to dictate your actions.
You forget who you are,
forget you can fly.

With the smell of burnt ashes
in your soul,
you continue to eat,
but this time,
it is to dull the pain…

III.

The flame awakens.
Something ignites the spark.
Once again, you burn
from deep inside.
At first, it's refreshing
and you fan the flame
with plans and ideas.
You even accomplish something
and it feels so good.

Then one thing
gets in the way,
then another.
You have to put
your creativity on hold,
stop the flow of passion.

One more cycle complete,
you eat more and more
trying to appease a hunger
that will never
be satisfied
with food.

WHOOPS!

I wrote the poem
In pretty ink
Set upon the page
To read before
Two hundred or so
Stood upon the stage
And when the lights
Came up so bright
And I looked upon my write
Surprise and shocked beyond belief
I found the paper white!

I had a wonderful opportunity to go on a cruise and they always have a talent show. I wrote a poem and decided to enter the contest. I love working with the colors of gel pens, but was shocked to discover that under bright lights they become invisible. I never memorize poems and after a few moments of panic, found that by angling the page, I was able to make out the words. Whew, that would've been embarrassing!

(I did not take this photograph.)

CHAPTER 4: RELATIONSHIPS---

SELF, OTHERS, AND SPIRIT

Priceless Expression

    This was an interesting chapter to put together. Here are poems inspired by situations, other people, or just in thinking about the person I am. A couple of poems came to me when I belonged to an on-line group called Perceptions of Life where there was talk of duality, illusion, and a relationship with the Beloved.

    I have fallen in, cried and bled in the pettiness of daily life. I have soared to heights that hold no explanations. Understand, that sometimes in the opening of the self, what comes through is often mystical, un-ordinary, and once in awhile, a place is reached in the soul that holds no bounds---
becoming
One with All That Is---
for a moment, anyway.

"I THINK THEREFORE…"

It started before this
and sometimes
I think it has always
been this way

I never noticed before
never paid attention
these glimpses of who I am
…always alone

there is light
there is dark
there is gray
one fades into the next

I strive to belong
in a world of chaos
but I am pulled off center
by always wanting
to fit in

Deep down I know
I will never find harmony
until I am willing
to let go of the desire
to be something
I am not

Deep down I know
I will never be at peace
until I accept
that I am…

ACCUSATIONS

Between the good times
A battle raged
You accused me
Of not listening
I accused you
Of not speaking up

Bouts of intense silence
Moments of angry scowls
Tight lipped immobility

Then a new dawning
As what you said
Sunk in
"You don't listen to me"
And a shocking
Realization
That I don't

In fear
Of a few
Hurtful words
I have shut down
To them all.

BURN

Roaring flames
Burn
Images of bodies
Flicker in firelight
Burn
Silent screams
Daily struggles
Trying to make sense
Of the corporate world
Burn
Singed eyebrows
Burnt hair
Looked too close
Burn
Fried brain
Tongue parched
Pushed to the limit
Burn

I, seemingly, alone
Surrounded by flame
Throw buckets
Of unshed tears
On the fiery walls
Watch dreams
Go up in smoke
Burn
Reach through flames
Fingers blister
Watch others' lives
Turn to ashes
Burn

I cannot save them
I cannot save my own
Burn.

CLINGING TO MEMORY

Warm hands cover my own
back to back we sit
on the dune
each lost in thought

I don't want to lose
this memory, this closeness
this feeling of being loved
if ever I was loved
and wondering if
I could ever be loved again

I don't want to lose
this memory, this feeling
because I am afraid
I may never get the chance
to experience
love again

Arms around me
holding eachother tight
a last goodbye hug
a kiss to my hair
I let go and turn away
before I burst into tears

CRAVING VALIDATIONS

Guilt falls soft
as I marvel
at the fact
that my soul
so craves
validation

I suck it up
as if it purges
negativity
from my heart
and I lay
in a drunken pool
of sweet praise

Renewed
I thank
the hundred
little gods
for your love

A friend once told me that because she has self confidence she doesn't need other people to validate her. Her statement made me think and question my own need.

ODE TO MY FRIENDS

I gather validations
as if they
are the only
proof
I am alive

I gather sweet accolades
as if I need
corroboration
of my worth

I gather your words
as if they give me
life supporting
oxygen

I gather your love
as if I
could not go on
without it

I gather you in my heart
You, who give me strength
You, who teach me love
You, who let me know
I am not alone.

ECHO OF DAYS GONE BY

She could not tell me
When tears turned blue
And I could not tell her
When sound turned pink

That summer on the hillside
Marked another change in time
And neither of us
Would ever be the same

Yet as we wandered
Through brown eyed Susans
And queen Anne's lace
Remembering the simplicity
Of childhood summers
I thought I heard
An angel cry

Like an echo
Of days gone by
We again said
Our farewells
Just as we had
Thirty years before

Her tears turned blue
And the sound of pink
Rang through my ears.

FLOYD'S WRATH

Up here
in my third floor loft
I am almost even
with the thrashing tree tops
rain pummels windows
wind howls through screens
echoes down chimneys
but, I, for once,
am safe and warm

Viewing without feeling
so much a part
of my detached life
that the very thought
of venturing outside
terrifies me

I, who once loved storms
would stand on barren hillside
while the wild winds
had their way with me,
now cower in fear
of just what opening
to that tremendous power
might mean

For surely if I let it
I would be filled once more
and the ferocious energies
would make me a wild woman

I tried it once
let the hurricane-force winds
tear through my soul
and in those few moments
I became more alive
than ever before

Glorious! Magnificent! Powerful!
I felt everything
saw everything
vivid, new, exciting

But They did not understand
the tiger was beaten, caged
and in the ensuing years
the face grew immobile
til the invisible bars
mattered no longer

Except when the winds
blow fierce
and I remember

FUTURE'S PAST

I lie in bed
Listening
To the boom, boom
Of the fireworks
In the distance

Morning finds me
Walking the lonely beach
Strewn with debris
From last night's
Aerial display

I wonder if
The twenty minute
Light show
Justifies
Littered sands,
It the beauty
Of a sunrise
Excuses
Empty beer cans
And cigarette butts

Or if eyes to the sky
Matters more than
Feet on the streets,
If beauty's importance
Is seen in spaces
So far ahead
That in the presence
Of today
The Earth
Holds such little wealth

What then, Mordecai
If tomorrow
Is more important
Than today?

I GIVE WITH JOY

My body, my hand, my soul
what is it that reaches
through space and time
to touch and feel?

How is it
that your heart
touches mine
without physical
contact?

Why do you
tear pieces
from my being
and scatter them
through space
as if I were a
rose?

But I am not
a rose.

Yet I shall give and give
words and love
until I am spent
and my seeds
are scattered
in the wind
like chaff

I shall love and love
until there is
nothing left
to love
and my petals
will be laid to rest
in the dirt
of someone else's
garden

I don't ever expect to be famous and I don't charge a lot for what I do, but every so often, someone will say that my words have inspired them. That response means more to me than money. If my words become the petals and seeds in someone else's garden and that person can become more joyful and creative, then I ask for nothing more.

NO EXCUSE!

Wasted energy
empty words upon
empty feelings
blockages to
truth and light
and the pain
written in your face
slapped against
my heart

Humiliation
came slow as
unshed tears
dried on parched lips
after leaving
hollow trails
forever etched
on my cheeks

My own words
flipped without care
in that moment
of frustration
lost credence
as the real world,
the natural world
enveloped me
in a blanket
of forgiveness and love

Still, that's
no excuse!
Saying I'm sorry
doesn't make it right
I regret
speaking
so thoughtlessly
in the first place
.

I took my anger and frustration out on the first person to come near. I will never forget the look on his face when I unleashed. I told myself that I could apologize later, and when I did, the pain still visible on him shook me. Why did I ever think saying, "I'm sorry," would make everything all right? In that moment, I realized that "I'm sorry" cannot erase the pain that hurtful words cause.

OPEN HEART SURGERY

That day
Sitting on the bench
As the leaves
Around us
Turned yellow
Felt like
Delicate surgery
As we tried
To suture
The wounds
Of many years

Best friends
Chosen sisters
Trying to heal
The betrayal
Caused by adults
Who pulled
Us apart
So many years
Ago

We searched
Carefully
For words
To soothe
The scars,
Strengthen
The friendship,
And rekindle
The flame
Of love
That never
Totally
Died.

PIECES OF YOU

The words fall forth
From silver tongues
And I gather them
To my page as if
It's a matter
Of life and death

To me…it is
It has been
And I pick
The fragments over
Searching for gold

Then rediscover
Myself
In the reflections
Leftover from
Pieces of
You.

REMEMBERED SOUNDS

Waves pounding
wake me
from my dreams

Where yesterday
is remembered
in the clear sparkle
of your eyes
and the shine
in your hair

I remember you
telling me
that nothing
lasts forever
That love, infinite
cannot be poured
into one shell

I remember the sounds;
the echo of your voice
the closing of the door
I fell back to sleep
listening
as my heart
beat louder
than the surf

RESPONSE

In the middle
of a hundred and one
messages,
a pause

words once more
pull me in
I cannot get away
nor do I want to

what I want
is to live here

how can I turn
my back on each write
how can I not feel
the essence of your thoughts
when I am You

I want to respond
to each piece
I want to touch
each individual soul
I want you to know
that I love you

Hear my words
and let the fingers
of my heart
wrap yours
in the deepest
respect and honor

Beloveds
I want to save
each poem
each thought
each you

Instead
of wasting paper
I have named
the flowers
in my garden
after you

SAVORED WORDS

I want to savor these words
roll them over my tongue
taste their sweetness
feel the light
trickle down my throat
with each swallow

Oh, to be loved so,
waking up
to precious thought
each day
breakfasting on the love
of those searching
for self truth,
of those having the courage
to bare their souls
for love

I am a simple spider
sharing Mira's web
rejoicing with
the opportunity
to spin my own threads

My tongue laps
each essence
and the fragrance
of the Beloved
is in my heart

I become you.

SEE NO EVIL

Big corporations
little corporations
America
the industrialized
mechanized
computerized
super-country

Where life is run
by the clock
where names
have given way
to numbers

Numbers for everything
employee numbers
telephone numbers
social security numbers
credit card numbers
license, registration and
account numbers

Too easy
to not get involved
personally

So when your number
is pulled from the file
everyone else
turns their head
and thanks God
it's not them

TELL ME

Tell me about this hunger
that food cannot satisfy

how no matter how good
the meal, something is still

missing. Tell me of this
yearning in your soul

that feeds on your thoughts
churning them like butter

till there is a creamed
texture and you can't tell

one ingredient from the
next. Tell me of the ache

that never goes away, the
one that haunts your dreams

while you lay in bed at night
under moon glow shining through
your window. Tell me why my
heart cries tears my eyes cannot

shed and I will tell you
why we are alone.

THE GATHERING

My heart cannot hold the words
If I do not write them, say them
They are forever lost
But my tongue
Does not speak my heart
I stutter, flustered
Surfaced emotions
Fill the throat
Cut off the voice

Words riddled
With sobs
Lose their meaning
I cannot say
I love you
For fear of seeing
Rejection written
Across your faces

You gather me
To your arms
And within these
Open hearts
and mingled tears
We become One

"...THEREFORE I AM"

Tell me about this alone space
How I wanted it
And now that I have it
I am scared

Tell me how to be
When all I have ever known
Is what I am not

Tell me why the sadness
Will never abate
Why I will forever wait
For Someone who will not come

Yesterday will never return
And I would not wish it
But perhaps there is
Something to be said
About ignorance

No, don't tell me
What I already know
I will learn to be grateful
For what I have… am.

CHAPTER 5: IN MEDITATION

    Of course I have to include a section on the poems that come to me through meditations and the practices of Tai Chi. I explore the deepest depths of my soul, then let it all go. The focus narrows and openness expands. I consider distractions and accept even those as part of the process.

BEYOND SILENCE

There is a silence
between a child's cry
and the crinkling
of cellophane

to go there
I have to forget
I am here

to stay there
I have to forget
I am me

Once there
memory must
cease

In the silence
between sounds
I become
a million stars
and time
no longer exists

EMBRACE

I wanted to shun
Rumi
when he talked
of God

but his words
wrapped around
my soul
and his soul
wrapped around
my heart

I knew what
he was saying
before I read
the words
my pounding heart
slowed
my mouth
going dry

How did he know
I would feel
this way
and I would
welcome the God
I no longer
called mine?

EXPLORING EMPTINESS

Let the emptiness approach
Slowly, secretively
Let it tempt you, seduce you

Slip inside that space
As if sliding your tongue
Between the soft, wet lips
Of a dew-covered lady slipper

With no expectations
Ride the feathers of nothingness
Pay soft attention to sighs
Breathe in… breathe out…

Take note of patterns
Let the "fingers" of your mind's eye
Wander over textures

Let sight and sound
Come to you
As a lazy stream meandering through
An undeveloped forest

Let the waters of emptiness
Lap your gentle shores

INSOMNIA

In the darkest of night
I wake at odd hours
With an unnamed restlessness
Driving me from warm bed

Empty corridors
Are roamed in soft footfalls
While my mind chatters
In uncontrollable soliloquy

The question of why
Tears through my soul
Till by candlelight
The stark, white pages
Are filled with hopes,
Dreams and revelations

After all these years
Of wondering
I can finally
Put the question to rest

It's not so much
A problem of insomnia
It's that the darkness
Doesn't want to be
Alone.

LIGHTNING STRIKE

Ever since that night
When lightning's' residue
Coursed through
My body's cells
I now fear storms

That spark, that jolt
That left me
Quivering for hours
In my bed
Will forever remain
Etched on my soul

Ever since that night
My heart pounds
With each storm
Fearful of the pain
I did not feel
Fearful of the electricity
That shocked my being

Ever since that night
I fear that unknown
Part of me
That has yet
To awaken…
Because
It almost
Did.

PRE-DAWN TAI CHI

In the half light my hands move through
space as if floating on their own accord

I melt into the soft structured form
as gentleness flows through my body

I am the song in the hearts of twittering chickadees
and the opening of the daisy greeting the dawn

Gentle breath commands power to move
this physical bulk with simple grace

I am a ghost casting shadowy
images against a blank wall

and my hands are the tender reeds
blowing in a warm summer breeze

I rest in nothingness.

<u>SHOPPING</u>

This dream
that I've sometimes
called nightmare

This dream
I've often
called hard

This dream
that is reality
This reality
that is illusion

When I realized
I was homeless
I threw out
empty cans and old newspapers
from a life I no longer lived
and then,
I went shopping

STAND IN SILENCE

Stand in Silence
aware of our roots
extending deep into the Earth
drawing this energy
into our centers
aware of the heavens
gathering of golden light
drawing this energy
into our centers
strong, powerful
formed into a pearl
Stand in Silence.

The movement starts
and we become
the energy that moves us
we become the form
flowing, gentle
breath matching movement
we are one with the form
slow, slower
energy rising up
from the Earth
to flow to the tips
of our fingers
to be brought back down
again to our centers
We become lost in the form
minds and bodies
melding with the energy
that moves us, becomes us

Last push
energy flows through
fingertips
arms reach overhead
touched by heavenly light
downward arc
encircles the body
with a mixture
of Heaven and Earth energies
pulling up to the heart
settling down into center
leaving us to
Stand in Silence.

TELLING

Tell me about the space
Between meditation and sleep
Tell me how if I become relaxed enough
Awareness can slip between
The sheets of reality

Tell me how if I maintain
Gentle awareness
And let go of expectations
Magic can happen

Don't tell me
It is not real
Don't tell me
Dreaming only happens
In the unconscious

I tell you
I've been there
I tell you
That I've walked the high wire
Between this world and that

I tell you
I've pulled back the veil
And dared to enter in

I tell you
I've come back…
Alive!

I.

Settling down
Relaxing body
Breathing deep

I step out
Spread the essence
Of pure cat-love
Into a world
Where few
Consciously travel

She,
Who teaches
Simple joy
Watches
From her chair
For me
To finish
My morning ritual
As if
Making sure
I do it
Right.

II.

I am nothing
I am everything
Nothing matters
Everything matters

One tiny grain
In this vast sand pile
Called universe
No feeling
Just being
Floating
In an endless void
Of space
Of potential

No feeling
No excitement
Nothing matters
But present moment
Everything matters
Because I am
About to step
Into total beingness
And I will
Never be the same.

VI.

Prayer
Meditation
Tai Chi
Contemplation

Early morning
Rituals
Performed
Before dawn

I am now
Ready
To face
The day.

VII.

Settled in silence
Sounds of the house
Wrap around me
Breathing in
Breathing out
My mind I bring
Down, down
Feel the spiral
Center my soul

Up, up
The rising spiral
Encompasses my heart
Feeds my mind
Continues its rise
Connecting
To the Universe

Then down, down
Once again
Sending the spiral
Deep into the Earth
Breathing in
Breathing out
Connecting
With All That Is

The emptiness
Of possibility
Astounds me
I wait patiently
Breathing in
Breathing out.

VIII.

Breathe out…
Expand, dissolve…
Breathe out…
Expand, dissolve…

Small, furry cat-ball
Stretched between
My knees
Lies across
My feet

Breathe out…
Expand…dissolve…

She teaches me
Simple love
Unconditional
Triangular face
Looks to me
With such
Gentleness
Such patience
I cannot help
But reach down
Scratch under
Her chin
Rub her belly
As she rolls over
Like a puppy

I return to focus
Breathe out…
Expand…dissolve…
Taking pure, gentle
Cat-love
Into the void.

IX.

Sitting
Cross-legged
Hard pillow
Underneath
Body relaxing
Candles flicker
Incense burns
Sandalwood,
Cedar, sage
Breathing deepens

Just when I think
I'm about to slip
Into another realm
She comes
Head butts my hand
For kitty pats
Lays on crossed ankles
Abetting the numbness
Then stretches
Full length
To place
One soft paw
On my lips

I gather her
Into my arms
Rub my cheek
To hers
She rubs back

Candles flicker
Incense burns
Breathing deepens
We meditate.

X.

Cross-legged
Hands on knees
Eyes closed
Breathing slowed
In…out…in…out…

Light from above
Showers me
In brilliance
I am emptied
I am filled

My face
Upward turns
I cannot stop it
Do not want to
This head
Not bowed
In shame
Nor obedience

This face looks
Openly, lovingly
To the glory
Of the heavens
Awesomeness
Of the universe
Beauty of the earth
The wonder
Of life

I breathe life
In…out…in…out…

XI.

Mother Theresa
Slipped into
My dreams
A name
A face
A smile

Perhaps
In my own search
For compassion
In a world
I perceived
As ruthless and
Unforgiving
She is but
A reminder
That only
A loving heart
Will make
Difference

My anger
And frustration
Are laid
At her feet
As I accept
My destiny.

XII.

A conscious
Effort
Me
To allow
My body
To sit
In a relaxed
State

I know
What I know
As into harmony
Flows
Mind, body,
Spirit

I love
What I see
When the woman
Returning
The mirror's
Gaze
Repulses me
So

Even though
I found
Her
Holding
Fresh picked
Lilies of the valley.

XIII. PURPOSE AND INTENT

With purpose and intent
Movement becomes graceful
Becomes meditative
Slowly…slowly…
Breathe softly
With each motion
With each step

Flow with
The sun's energy
Follow
The moon's path
Let the earth's
Cool, blue
Awaken each nerve
Allow light
To shine
In every crevice

Each movement
Is with purpose
As the meridians
Open to the flow
And pathways
Become renewed

Intent is
Everything
As I gather
This energy
Into my womb.

XIV.

Being present
Being attentive
Listening
Wide open

With luck
It may only take
A few more years
To obtain
Compassion
To hear
And not judge

But I've placed
One more piece
In the puzzle
And taken
One more step
In the journey
Of a thousand miles.

XV. THE WAITING

In the silence
Towards evening
Crickets keep tune
With distant traffic

So far, so near
And so many
Lifetimes away
I've sat
Waiting for you

Like a lover
Stealing a kiss
In the night
The breeze
Rustles a whisp
Of my hair
And my tears
Are carried away
In the chickadees' song

In the silence
The pain is released
Peace descends
Like a comforting blanket
And I wait
All night
For your coming

What joy it is
To see the sun rise!

XVI. LETTING GO IDENTITY

My life built of pieces
Of family, friends, lovers
Slowly pulled together
From a lifetime
Of hurts and joys

Self esteem on a soapbox
I faced the world saying
"This is who I am!"

Today a revelation
The layers of this
Carefully put together
Identity
Cracked and peeled

And I know now
That enlightenment
Can only be reached
By letting go
The very things
I worked so hard
To create

The next time I am asked
What I do, I shall reply
"Nothing. I am Nobody."

I love this poem! When I wrote it, I was very amazed at the last line, and yet, it felt so true: a big, "Wow!" for me. This was one of those times when I slipped into a moment of true enlightenment. However, I feel I need to explain because some people don't see it as such. That's okay. This is not about self sabotage or denial, but a great revelation! Through studies in Buddhism, Taoism, Shamanism and learning about ego versus self-esteem, I came to realize that none of this matters. It's rather ironic. I spent years working on self-esteem and learning to love the self only to discover that I can let it all go and know that I am no better or worse than anyone else. In one aspect, I say I am nobody, but on the other hand, I am Everybody. I am one tiny grain of sand which makes up a vast dune.

What does matter is how I live my life. I keep a positive attitude, try to do good, and work at remaining calm and at peace. I practice acceptance and awareness and forgive myself any faults. I don't need fancy titles to tell me that I am successful. I don't need to prove anything. I am alive and am grateful for the experiences in this life!

I AM nobody and I AM everything!
During moments of inner peace,
I am One With All That Is.
What more could one ask for...

XVII. WALKING MEDITATION

Gone is the arrogance, the anger
As we walk…
In…
Mindfulness…

Intent becomes our guide
Breath, our focus
Our awareness expands
Breathing in the beauty
That surrounds us
Till we, too, become aware
Of our own inherent beauty

Each soft foot fall
Becomes a step of
Love, honor, respect
Walking in mindful silence
Breathing into the earth
Total awareness
Gentle intent

In these moments
Sounds become more pronounced
Colors more enhanced
Touch more acute
Love, compassion and joy
Fill our hearts to overflowing
And we pass it on
In mindful silence.

XIX. CALLING WINDHORSE

Silent sunrise
Shadow gives way to light
Venus and Moon
Greet the dawn
Morning evolves from night

I am dark, now I am light
Dark, then once again light
Who will notice
This lonely star
In dawning's magnificent sight

Pounding hooves of yesterday
Windhorse answers the sorrow
I gather in this new found power
Creating today
To prepare the morrow

Opened to this freshened awareness
And when the time is right
The art of fearlessness
Becomes the weapon
For the fight

To truly escape
From all the bonds
That trap me in the dark
I realize that calling Windhorse
Will always
Ignite the spark.

This poem came from my studies into "Shambhala, The Sacred Path of the Warrior" and other works of Chogyam Trungpa.

CHAPTER 6: LETTING THE WORDS FLOW

The next ten poems are ones that poured out of me in one sitting. It was a release after an intense emotional state. At the time, I was dealing with my mother's poor health and real estate problems. I was drained, depressed and at my wits' end. Perhaps the poems came to relieve me from that downward spiral. The creative burst certainly brought my spirits up.

When words pour out, I get excited. Where do they come from? In the moment, I didn't question, just kept the pen moving. What was even more interesting was the cadence in the rhyming in the first two poems. I let go and followed the words to the page. Maybe my emotional despair stirred up hidden feelings from deep within and caused this seemingly inconsequential outburst.

#1 02/26/07

Whistle and thistle and unbelieve
below this lonely evergreen
for when I'd come
I'd been deceived
before the thistle
before the green
and now it's gone
another year
I'd like to say
I shed no tears
but sorrow widens
and runs so deep
with tomorrow another
day to keep

2 FEB262007

Up and down
the road he swore
paced right up
to my front door
I watched him
from a window pane
as he ran back
down again
I wondered what
I'd done wrong
to make him stay
away so long
and lest my lover
forget to return
I'll leave unlocked
my heart to burn
what is this courting
oh, I don't know
but I wait impatient
for the Beloved to show

3 Feb262007

I couldn't light the night
with your words
I couldn't quench the flame
with your touch
your invisible hands
squeezed my throat
and all I could do
was stare into
your dark, hollow eyes

4 FEB262007

Flesh eats flesh
survival isn't only
for the fittest
I recall the night
you slipped away
I pretended not to notice

Flesh eats flesh
I want to live
in my own way
determined I am
to prove you wrong
I intend not to be fit

(by others' terms.)

5 FEB262007

It is inevitable
that poetry
can only come from
intense pain,
intense love,
intense joy,
intense sorrow

Take me as I am
let me cry
into your joy
Take your joy
let me join
with you in laughter
Take my sorrow
and love me forever
Take your pain
and I will wipe your tears
with my kisses

Oh, Beloved
lest I forget
what it was like
to be loved
return to me

6 FEB262007

Shannon called
Ross brought black sheep
over the meadow
Stars fell that day
touched the grasses
in early morning dew
which the lambs
lapped up
in the silence
of the dawn

*The above poem was **really** one of those bits where I had NO IDEA where the words came from or the picture in my mind that went along with it.*

7 FEB262007

This veil that grew
between me and thee
can only be remembered
on the tip of my tongue
I spit it out
like watermelon seeds
against the wind

8 FEB262007

I understand
this need, this lust
for words that
bed down in my soul
I understand
this need, this ache
that rips my soul
from end to end
til everything spills
EVERYTHING
that ever meant
anything

I understand
this pain, this drive
that causes me to
fall to my knees
and cry out
to the Gods
I understand
this intensity of love
that wrings words
from a soul
unable to speak
in plain English

9 FEB262007

March will come in
like a dead lover
and I, who can't even
wait to hear from you,
shall continue to shiver
from this emotional
downpour
Sorrow creeps under
my tongue and words
form paste in my mouth
I am suffocating
in this gloom
this cold through
gritted teeth
chills my brain
and freezes tears
on the inside
of my cheeks

You didn't have
to tell me
I knew the moment
you strayed from my side
You didn't have
to show me
I knew I would end up alone
with lonely thoughts
and lonely hours
and a lonely heart
longing to kiss
the upside of the moon

10 FEB262007

Fortunes creep
passion deep
with my mother's hand
I'll keep
watching for a chance
to sleep

Cradle rocked
mind unblocked
secrets that I once
forgot
sneak upon a heart
unlocked

'morrow's waiting
chances trading
I sit upon the lovelight
fading
never more to be one's
mating

Restless heart
longs for spark
idle hands and silent
bark
look upon a soul gone
dark

Comes the dawn
night has gone
I lay my soul upon
the lawn
wait for a message
from beyond

Beloved's worth
full of mirth
I feel the richness of
the earth
and like a mother, She gives
new birth

IN CLOSING

PURPOSE

Step softly
speak quietly
the wisdom
of life

Woman changes
woman courageous
studies
the night

In dreams
she wanders
green fields
full of clover

'Cross skies
she whispers
til gentleness
takes over

The morrow
steals quickly
yesterday's
dull reminders

Gray clouds
wash briefly
as rain falls
behind Her

Sun's warmth
moon brightness
from season to
season

Til time
signals endings,
death calls…
life ceases

THEY WILL NEVER WRITE SONGS ABOUT ME

Sometimes I feel so insignificant
so useless, so unimportant.
I am certainly nobody's hero,
never one to be looked up to
never to stand out in a crowd.
I will never Be somebody.
I am destined to stand in periphery
and They will never ever write songs about me.

Sometimes I get a glimpse beyond;
a glimpse, a fragile glimpse
of parted curtain, thinning veil.
What is it I see beyond the beyond?
clouded view of what could be,
cannot tell if it's really me;
fear pulls the shade, no longer free,
and They will never ever write songs about me.

At times I am uncomfortable
when I look upon myself.
Who do I think I am
to dream I can be different?
So I continue to live in shadow
hovering between fear and wanna be.
I know that no one will ever see,
know too, They will never write songs about me.

But to know I have a purpose
in the Greater Scheme of Life,
to decide to make my stand,
to know I have a choice.
I Am one who lives in both worlds,
I guess it's my destiny
living in the periphery
is why They will never write songs about me.

Out of the well of darkness
of heartache and despair,
comes words to release the pain, the grief
and it's these I wish to share
fame and fortune care not for me
open heart, open hand for all to see
letting everyone know it's okay with me
that They will never ever write songs about me.

This is my "signature" poem which I had self- published in 1995, and at the last minute, I feel compelled to include it here. It came to me after an intense teacher-training workshop and subsequent three month depression. Again, it was a great release. This is me and over 10 years later I cannot read it aloud without tears. I am very proud of this poem.

ABOUT THE AUTHOR

Sasha has lived in New Hampshire most her life. After high school, she spent almost thirty years in a local factory where she learned a lot about the manufacturing business. She worked many jobs from production to shipping. The later years found her in charge of purchasing and receiving in the stockroom and it was during those times that she began studying various healing arts and writing poetry.

Sasha graduated from the New Hampshire Institute of Therapeutic Arts in 1988 where she learned many hands-on healing techniques and a few years later, received a teaching certificate from Master Mantak Chia of the Healing Tao Association which permitted her to teach meditations and Tai Chi. In the late 1990s, Sasha took lessons in Peer Leadership Training and began leading support groups. She received a certificate in Cosmic Healing from Master Chia in 1998. In 2007, she became an Ordained Healing Minister.

Sasha's eclectic studies include Native American shamanism and she has read many books on Buddhism, Taoism, Wiccan, and Shambhala. She believes that these combined workings help her walk in beauty and harmony.

Throughout the years, writing has been Sasha's salvation. Writing is the outlet when life gets in the way of doing art and the daily journaling has allowed her to explore the inner turmoil which is often the precursor to the poems. That release onto the page brings a greater understanding and enjoyment of life.

> "I write because I have to.
> If I didn't, I'd die… or go crazy… or worse…"
> ----Sasha Wolfe

Sasha currently lives in Bradford, NH with her mom and her phenomenal cat, Freyja. She has published two books of poetry, had her poems in newsletters and anthologies, and received an Editor's Choice Award from the International Library of Poetry. A multi-talented woman, she is also a photographer and an artist.

Check out some of her other work at www.sashawolfe.net.

www.ingramcontent.com/pod-product-compliance
Lightning Source LLC
Chambersburg PA
CBHW040911020526
44116CB00026B/31